Rising Stars

How To Grow Your Audience, Your Business, And Your Revenue By Creating Short, Captivating Videos About Your Everyday Life With YouTube Marketing (With Actionable Tips To Follow From Successful Youtubers)

Justin A. Parker

Bluesource And Friends

This book is brought to you by Bluesource And Friends, a happy book publishing company.

Our motto is **"Happiness Within Pages"**

We promise to deliver amazing value to readers with our books.

We also appreciate honest book reviews from our readers.

Connect with us on our Facebook page www.facebook.com/bluesourceandfriends and stay tuned to our latest book promotions and free giveaways.

Don't forget to claim your FREE books!

Brain Teasers:

https://tinyurl.com/karenbrainteasers

Harry Potter Trivia:

https://tinyurl.com/wizardworldtrivia

Sherlock Puzzle Book (Volume 2)

https://tinyurl.com/Sherlockpuzzlebook2

Also check out our other books

"67 Lateral Thinking Puzzles"

https://tinyurl.com/thinkingandriddles

"Rookstorm Online Saga"

https://tinyurl.com/rookstorm

"Korman's Prayer"

https://tinyurl.com/kormanprayer

"The Convergence"

https://tinyurl.com/bloodcavefiction

"The Hardest Sudokos In Existence (Ranked As The Hardest Sudoku Collection Available In The Western World)"

https://tinyurl.com/MasakiSudoku

Table of Contents

Description

YouTube is a very large platform, and it can sometimes be difficult to figure out exactly where the spotlight is and how to attract it. With a reported average of over 400 hours of video content uploaded every minute, it can be a daunting task to find success on this platform. This book is, however, designed to guide you on the path to that success. *How To Grow Your Audience, Your Business, And Your Revenue By Creating Captivating Videos About Your Everyday Life With YouTube Marketing (With Actionable Tips To Follow From Successful YouTubers)* will help you to understand YouTube's algorithms and to utilize them and the systems that they have implemented in order to build your brand and maximize your potential on this platform.

In order to do this, however, you will first need to understand the service that you are providing and how to cater that service to those who are most likely to consume the content that you produce and continue to consume the content that you put out. Maintaining these "repeat customers" is the key to building a consistent fanbase and growing that fanbase even further. Businesses like the ones that exist on platforms like YouTube are built on audience retention and dedicated followings. Word-of-mouth advertising is the most powerful tool that new and/or growing businesses have, especially ones that exist within the Internet, simply due to the sheer amount of content that exists within it. YouTube alone had over 1.3 billion users as of 2017, and as of right now, an estimated total of as many as 2 billion users. The platform reports an average of 400 hours of video content being uploaded every minute. With a constantly and consistently increasing amount of content on the platform, it is literally impossible to calculate the total amount of content, measured in their duration, that exists on YouTube. Because of both the incalculable amount of content as well as the extremely large user base, it can be very challenging to develop a clear presence that stands out above the crowd and attracts new viewers. Luckily, however, there are some handy tips, tricks, and shortcuts that can help you to do just that.

This can be a very difficult, time-consuming, and mentally exhausting task, but *How To Grow Your Audience, Your Business, And Your Revenue By Creating Captivating Videos About Your Everyday Life With YouTube Marketing* is designed to help you understand your brand and target audience and use that knowledge along with the knowledge of your product, and the type of content that you are aiming to put out to help you formulate interesting and engaging videos that will help you to attract and keep consistent, dedicated viewers and follower bases in order to find a foothold in the YouTube market and eventually carve out your own path From there, you can then build a legitimate career in content creation.

Rising Stars

Introduction

I would like to thank you for taking the initiative to build your business and your channel on YouTube by purchasing this copy of my book, *How To Grow Your Audience, Your Business, And Your Revenue By Creating Captivating Videos About Your Everyday Life With YouTube Marketing (With Actionable Tips To Follow From Successful YouTubers)*.

I would also like to extend a short word of congratulations for taking the first few steps on the path to stepping out on to the "stage" of having internet presence and taking the time to learn the most effective ways and methods to build your presence online. This book is designed to help you develop all of the tools necessary to become a successful creator of high-quality content on YouTube. I am informing you about the topics that will help you to do so by showing you how to develop various skills that are necessary for this goal.

Of course, this book is specifically designed to act as a guide in helping you to understand how YouTube functions, all of its very complicated algorithms, as well as the various tools that you can use to maximize your potential on this incredibly popular platform. It is also meant to help you utilize these tools and the systems that YouTube uses, to sort all of the content that is stored within itself in order to benefit yourself and to help you find success on this site. In order to accomplish this lofty goal, however, you will first need to evaluate and understand the service or services that you are able to provide to your audience, and how you can tailor your content, or "service", to the people who are the most likely to consume the content that you produce, and then upload it to your YouTube channel. Understanding your brand and being able to maintain these kinds of "repeat customers" is the key to beginning to build a consistent audience and fanbase, and beginning to build and grow that fanbase even further. Businesses like the kind that exist on online platforms like YouTube are built on the concept of audience retention and on consistent and dedicated followers and "fans." One of the most powerful and useful tools that new and/or growing businesses have access to and can utilize effectively is called "word-of-mouth" advertising. This can be described as an unpaid or free form of advertisement or promotion that involves the act of satisfied "customers" (or viewers, in the case of YouTube channels and other forms of entertainment media) telling their friends and the people they know about their experiences with a particular business, as well as their products and services. This "word-of-mouth" advertising can be incredibly important for every type of business, especially new ones that are trying to build their brand, as it is based on happy customers helping your business by directing new customers and patrons toward your business and informing them about the services or products that you and your business can provide.

This type of "word-of-mouth" advertising is one of the most useful and powerful tools that a new or growing business can use to help them to grow and become more successful. This applies especially for new Internet businesses, simply due to the amount of unique content that exists within it. YouTube alone had over 1.3 billion individual users on its site as of 2017, and as of right now, the site has gained even more users, with a number that is estimated to have around 2 billion unique active users. This incredibly popular platform reports that it has an average of 400 or more hours of video content uploaded every minute.

With a constantly and consistently increasing amount of content on the platform, it is literally impossible for anyone to even begin to calculate the total amount, measured in either their duration or even just the number of videos, that exists on YouTube. Because of both the seemingly impossibly large and incalculable content as well as the sites' extremely large and constantly increasing number of individual users, it can be very difficult and challenging for new content creators to begin to develop a clear presence that can stand out among the crowd and attract new viewers. Luckily, however, there are a handful of very useful tips, tricks, and various shortcuts that can help you to accomplish that goal and find success on YouTube.

This can be a very difficult, time-consuming, and mentally exhausting task, but *How To Grow Your Audience, Your Business, And Your Revenue By Creating Captivating Videos About Your Everyday Life With YouTube Marketing (With Actionable Tips To Follow From Successful YouTubers)* is designed to help you in accomplishing this goal by acting as a guide on the path to learning how to understand and develop your brand and target audience and use that knowledge along with the knowledge of your product or service, which is the type of content that you are aiming to create and put on your YouTube channel, to help you formulate your own unique and original, interesting and engaging videos that can serve to help you to attract and keep consistent, dedicated viewers and follower bases in order to find a strong foothold in the "YouTube market" and eventually carve out your own path, and from there, build a legitimate and successful career in YouTube content creation.

Section 1: Conceptualization

This first section of *How To Grow Your Audience, Your Business, And Your Revenue By Creating Captivating Videos About Your Everyday Life With YouTube Marketing (With Actionable Tips To Follow From Successful YouTubers)* will be about the first chronological step in this process, which will be referred to as "conceptualization." Conceptualization, as it is discussed here, will be referred to in the context of building a successful and entertaining YouTube channel that will help you to build a business and a brand that will appeal to your audience and help you to, again, become more successful. This chapter will go over various topics related to this idea of "conceptualization", such as the visualization of your unique brand, identifying and understanding the interests of your audience and the products or services that you can provide to that audience, and using that knowledge to help you in order to determine your "niche" or your place in the "YouTube market."

Of course, it can also seem at a surface level to be somewhat counterproductive to put off the sort of things that will be immediately helpful to us and to our businesses that involve taking a more active and direct action in favor of passivity. It can, however, be very important, and even vital to your success and the success of your business and brand, to stop and take a moment to understand your goals and aspirations, and how they can be related to your business and the type of products and services that you can provide to your audience through that business.

Having a concrete plan of action for yourself and your channel, and by extension, your business, will ultimately be incredibly helpful for you on the way to achieving these goals that you have set for yourself. If you do not have a plan written out as a guide for yourself when you are executing these sorts of public endeavors, they can begin to seem very discordant or chaotic, and can then begin to become much more difficult for you to achieve than they otherwise would have been if you had prepared for them beforehand. For example, the content that you choose to create might end up being a little bit too varied for your audience or viewership to completely understand. You might begin to notice yourself jumping from one topic to another, and shifting these topics back and forth from video to video. With no set structure or guideline to follow, it can become a little bit more difficult for your viewers to pin down the type of content that they can expect. Additionally, this can also make it somewhat difficult for viewers to easily access your content from a consumer's point of view. This section and the chapters within it will help you with these kinds of more sensitive topics, and give you all of the tools that will be necessary in order to help you to find success on YouTube and to accomplish the goals that you set for yourself.

Chapter 1: Visualizing Your Brand

The first step, and arguably one of the most important ones that you should take on the long path toward the goal of building a successful and entertaining channel and business on YouTube, as the name of this chapter would suggest, is for you to begin visualizing your brand. What it means to "visualize your brand", putting it in simple terms, is for you to form a clear and specific image in your mind of the specific type of content that you want to produce and put up onto your channel on YouTube in order to help you to grow your brand and your business. This also involves the ability to understand the images and the messages that you would like to project onto each of the products that you create. This sort of projection of your thoughts and ideas, as well as your opinions, feelings, and emotions, is absolutely inevitable, and will most definitely be present and apparent to those that are looking for them in anything that you create, no matter how hard you may be trying to mask or hide them. Your personality and your mannerisms will be apparent in anything that you create, whether it is public or private in nature. It is completely and absolutely inevitable that you will sort of "bleed" into everything you create. If you try to treat each video as if it were a full-length film, it will then become much easier for you to begin understanding this difficult concept. When you consider the various types of films that certain individual people or groups of people produce, or all of the different actors in those various films and the way they handle their roles, you can usually see those people, especially if you are looking for the actors' "real life" personalities and mannerisms in their creations, with no exceptions. This includes all of the various aspects of a person's personality, such as their sense of humor, their mannerisms, their likes, and their dislikes.

Because of this evident inevitability, you will need to consider these things about yourself in order to understand how these aspects of your personality will "shine through" your videos, and manage how they will manifest and the extent to which they do as well. You will need to try to understand all of the aspects of yourself and your own personality and mannerisms that you have that are marketable, and can or will either attract or repel any new or even older viewers and consumers of your brand and your content that you produce on YouTube. You will need to look inward and begin to evaluate yourself in order to understand all of these qualities before you can attempt to do anything else. This will help you to understand a lot of the more subtle ways in which you will either intentionally or unintentionally affect all of the content that you create on YouTube, and will allow you to control it more effectively, and in ways that can even be beneficial to both you and the things that you create. It will make it a lot easier for you to incorporate all of those positive aspects of your personality, such as your sense of humor and your interests, while also being able to choose to exclude the ones that you think might not be so positive, interesting, or entertaining to your audience. This is the first thing that you will need to do in search of this goal of becoming successful on YouTube. Figure out which qualities that you have that might be interesting or entertaining from the point of view of the people who will potentially be consuming your content, and by extension, your personality, and your quirks—or at least the aspects of those qualities that you will choose to project onto the videos and any other content that you produce.

Once you have done this, of course, you will then want to use the knowledge of the aspects of your personality that you believe to be interesting or entertaining to narrow down your specific "brand." This means that you will need to understand exactly how people will perceive you and your brand based on your appearance, mannerisms, humor, and anything else that you might end up weaving into your content in order to form a clearer and more accurate image of, coincidentally, your image. Specifically, this will affect your image through the eyes of your viewers. You may even be able to manipulate this image, if you choose to do so, to allow you to include certain aspects of your personality, while also excluding others that you would prefer to leave your viewers in the dark about. This can be very important for the sake of maintaining a positive "political" image, of sorts. It can be incredibly difficult to do so, however, if you make a lot of exceptions very suddenly or without any sort of direct warning to your viewers. This can surprise your viewers, and convince them that you may be dishonest or untrustworthy, which might be particularly bad for business if honesty or even accuracy is an important aspect of your "brand."

The most important thing to consider is how certain aspects of your personality fit in with the image that you wish to project in your content, and how you would like to be perceived, both in relation to yourself and your creations. If you attempt to piece together a lot of wildly disorganized and discordant topics, opinions, or even mannerisms, your content can project a sort of "cognitive dissonance". This can make it very difficult for your viewers to understand the meaning of your videos, how you might feel about certain topics or subjects, or even various aspects of your basic personality. Many individuals will choose to explicitly disclose that they tend to put up a "stage persona," or wear a "mask" of sorts in order to make more interesting videos and other content. This can be very beneficial for established content creators, especially for ones that improvise their videos or create any kind of "behind the scenes" content that show an aspect or various different aspects of their personality that might contradict previous content that they have already been released in the past.

Once you have gained a more complete understanding of these different and very important concepts, however, you will then be able to more effectively and accurately control the different kinds of content that you produce. This helps you best suit the specific brand that you wish to follow, and you will then project this onto all of your other videos to create the best type of content for your particular audience.

Chapter 2: Identifying Your Audience

This chapter will cover a concept that is very similar and somewhat connected to the one discussed in the first chapter of this book. This second chapter will be all about the concept of "identifying your audience", which will be the next step to take once you've found your channel's specific brand, and obtained a clear image of exactly how you would like to be perceived by your audience with regards to all of the content that you will produce for your YouTube channel and your brand as a whole. Another really good way that you can look at the task of identifying your audience is as another part of understanding exactly how people will perceive you and your brand, as the people who will enjoy your content are obviously also going to be much more likely to continue to consume the content in the future. These are both, however, distinct parts of the larger goal of conceptualizing your product. This knowledge that you acquire regarding the topics that will be covered in each of these chapters will eventually be needed to factor in to all of the decisions that you will make that will affect your videos on an individual basis and any potential guidelines you might end up setting for yourself about the specific type of content you will produce. It will also be very important for you to take note of this information when you are creating any icons and graphics of any sort, whether they will be created by you, or by any other individual who you might collaborate with for your channel on YouTube, as well as for your business and brand. It might even be arguable that this knowledge can be even more important for these reasons if you do not create these graphics yourself, but instead hire another person to create these kinds of graphics for you and your YouTube channel. If you hire another individual to do these kinds of things, then you will also need to be able to accurately and effectively convey to them the concepts and ideas that you might have for your brand and your channel on YouTube, as well as the various different types of images that you might require. You need to convey it in such a way that this other person will be able to understand and translate it for you easily.

Being able to effectively and easily identify and understand your audience can be incredibly important in order to build a successful business as well, because it will then allow you to use all of the knowledge of your own personality and of your brand to effectively and efficiently design and market all of the different content within your videos much more effectively than you would otherwise be able to do if you did not have this understanding. If you are already familiar with the type of people who would be consuming your content, it will then become much easier for you to create high-quality content that will be of interest to all of those people. This will in turn maximize their satisfaction with your content, their levels of entertainment, leading to greater success in your creation of interesting content on YouTube. This will then allow you to continue to grow your channel and business and make more videos that are interesting to both you as well as your viewers.

As the second part of the section of this book on conceptualization, the concept of understanding your audience and the people who will be consuming the content that you create will need to be done alongside the task of visualizing your brand, and understanding the products and services that you can provide to that audience. It will also be much easier for you to know what kind of people may end up consuming the content that you produce for your channel on YouTube if you understand what the product actually is to begin with, after all. These two very important tasks, as well as the ones that will be covered in the next two chapters of this section, might even be carried out in portions and pieced together like a puzzle along the way. You might even end up deciding on a target audience, and then realizing that a certain aspect or aspects of the videos that you have planned might not be completely appropriate for these groups of people. If this happens, you will then need to tweak the concept that you already have developed, and make adjustments in order to make it more appropriate for your audience. Or you may notice later down the line that you wish to create a new type of content altogether. At this point, you will need to ask yourself how you can market this new format to your current audience, or if you will need to branch out and attempt to expand your audience to include this new demographic.

As far as the actual task of "identifying your audience" goes, it is a fairly simple one: You will need to determine the types of people who will consume the content that you create. Who will your videos be entertaining to, and for what reason? You will need to produce videos that appeal to these people. In order to do so, you will first need to understand who you are creating your videos for. There are a few different ways to determine this. You might ask yourself who are the people who would be attracted to the brand you have created for yourself and your content, or you might ask what sort of people you would actually like to create content for, and proceed from there instead. Regardless of how you come to this conclusion, it will ultimately bring you one step closer to finding your success on YouTube and building your career in content creation. The next step on this road to success, of course, is to understand your value, and the specific skills and qualities that you bring to the table. The next chapter, which covers this exact concept, is called "Determining Your Niche."

Chapter 3: Determining Your Niche

The previous chapter was all about using the knowledge of your brand and the type of content that you would like to create in your videos on YouTube. This will help you to identify the kind of audience that you would like to create your videos for, and how these kinds of things can have a strong effect on the type of content that you will produce. This chapter of *How To Grow Your Audience, Your Business, And Your Revenue By Creating Captivating Videos About Your Everyday Life With YouTube Marketing* will be about using that information in order to gain a more specific understanding of your place in the eyes of a consumer on YouTube.

This chapter will cover a concept that is very similar to, and will be connected to the previous two that were discussed in the first and second chapters of this book. This third chapter is going to be all about the concept of "determining your niche," which is the next step that you will want to take on this path once you have figured out your specific brand, and have decided on the kind of audience that you will market your videos to. A very simple way to help you to understand this chapter's goal is for you to think of this goal in terms of your "product", and how you can market that product to the people who will end up consuming it. What specific service can you provide to the people who will choose to consume the content that you create? What will people be attracted to in each of your videos, specifically? As with each of the topics that have been covered in the previous chapters in this section as well as the next and last one, this chapter's task might need to be completed in tandem with the other parts of its section. It will also need to be considered during many of the later chapters as well, in order to maximize the effectiveness and efficiency of the pace at which you can absorb and understand them.

Being able to determine your niche can be described, in short, as the ability to gain an understanding of the specific service that you will be providing to your audience in your videos or other content, and how that service will be unique and able to stand out to your audience as compared to other similar content. This can be incredibly useful for helping you build a brand and understand your place in the "YouTube market," which will, in turn, bring you more success and allow you to continue to produce high-quality content that will be enjoyable and fulfilling for you and your viewers.

People seem to love to say, "You need a hook." This is true, to some degree. At a basic level, there needs to be a reason for a person to consume one particular product over another, especially if these products are very similar to each other. Having a specific service that you provide to your audience or the people who will be consuming the content that you create that others may not have can help you to become more noticeable and stand out in the sea of videos and channels on the platform and the Internet as a whole. As has been stated previously in this book's introduction, there are an estimated 400 or more hours of content that are uploaded to YouTube per minute on average. For this reason, it can be very difficult for you to be noticed on your own. It can be helpful, however, to spark some sort of discussion or discourse about the content that you create in order to generate interest in your videos and in your opinions, so that people will be more interested in the things you have to say. Word-of-mouth advertising is known to be one of the most effective methods there is, and will help you to bypass having to "force" people to find you in a sea of very similar videos if a specific video of yours is directly recommended to them by a friend whose opinion they already value and trust. Not only this, but it can also be helpful for you to show up higher on search engine rankings if some of your content is already receiving traffic. This will be discussed further in a later chapter on Search Engine Optimization.

As far as the actual task of "determining your niche" goes, you will need to determine the type of content you wish to create and consider what services you can provide that other similar creators cannot or do not provide themselves. What is it that sets you apart and that makes you unique? What is it about you and your content that will get people talking about you and the content that you create? These are the important questions to ask, especially at the start. Getting noticed by new viewers can be incredibly important and helpful in a new business, and a YouTube channel needs to be thought of as a "new business" in almost every way in order to succeed on the platform. Once you have determined the qualities that are present in yourself and in the videos that set you apart from other channels, videos, and services to be compared to, you can then use that information to help you to build your brand further. This will ultimately serve to bring you one more step closer to finding your success on YouTube, building your career in content creation. The next step on this road to success, of course, is to understand your value and the specific skills and qualities that you bring to the table. The next chapter, which covers this exact concept, is called "Understanding your Product." It will also be the last chapter in this section, and incorporate all of the information and concepts that have been discussed in the first two chapters as well as in this one.

Chapter 4: Understanding Your Product

The previous chapter in this book went over the very important topic of "understanding your niche". This was all about understanding the specific service that you can provide to your audience in your videos/other content, as well as how that service can differ from other channels/videos on YouTube that provide very similar services. You also learn how to stand out from the crowd. This chapter will be the last of four parts of the first section of *How To Grow Your Audience, Your Business, And Your Revenue By Creating Captivating Videos About Your Everyday Life With YouTube Marketing*, which has been designed to help you to prepare to begin your career on YouTube by conceptualizing the specific type of content that you wish to produce, and how it will be shaped by your own personality and quirks, as well as how you can cater that content to your target audience in a manner that they will find interesting and engaging. This chapter will go over the topic of "understanding your product", as well as how you can use the knowledge of the various topics that were discussed in previous chapters of this book in order to gain a more complete understanding of the specific type(s) of content that you will be producing when moving forward, and how that content should be handled as well. Each of these various topics will be relevant in many of the later chapters of this book, as it will be important to have a clear vision of these concepts in order for you to be able to execute your ideas as effectively as you can.

Being able to understand the product(s) that you create for your audience, basically means to use the knowledge of your particular brand and how you will be perceived by the people who are watching your videos/other content in order to share with them. As well, how you can make your created videos stand out in order to grow your viewership and audience even further so as to to find success with YouTube ultimately. As for the actual goal for this chapter, you will simply need to consider these factors and use them to help you to develop a clear idea of the type of content that you will produce, and the purpose of that content, with regards to the people who watch your videos. This can seem, at first glance like an easy task, but sometimes, it may not be so simple to do this. It can be incredibly challenging to find a sense of the sort of image that one might want to project publicly, and it can also be even more difficult to maintain that image while also avoiding creating dissonant impressions that can often leave viewers confused about the opinions or intentions of the creators of the content that they may consume. Once you have discovered a good balance of these concepts and ideas and how to manage them, it can become much simpler, and you will then be able to move on with greater ease to the next step.

The next section will be on "preparation", and will cover the more literal topics, such as the actual type of content that you will create, and the frequency that you will create that content, as well as the duration of your videos and why that can be incredibly important to your channel and your brand. This will help you attract and maintain a consistent viewership for your YouTube channel.

Section 2: Preparation

Congratulations! At this point, you should have finished the first section of *How To Grow Your Audience, Your Business, And Your Revenue By Creating Captivating Videos About Your Everyday Life With YouTube Marketing*! You should now have a clearer idea of the concepts and ideas that were talked about within the first section and its four chapters, such as being able to visualize your brand, identifying and understanding your audience, determining your niche, and understanding your product completely. With these skills, you should now have all the necessary tools for you to be able to move forward on the path to gaining a complete understanding of the concepts and ideas that will be covered in the remaining chapters of this book, and you will be well on your way to finding success on YouTube and finding a fulfilling and satisfying career in content creation on this platform.

This next section of this book is called "preparation", and it will cover more of the literal topics involved in the process of creating videos for your channel on YouTube, such as the actual type of content that you will create, as well as the frequency of your videos, and the duration of each of the videos that you will put out for your viewers, and why the duration of each of your videos can be so important in order to help you in maintaining a constant and consistent viewership, as well as the most optimal length of the videos for your audience in particular. These can be very important steps on the road to "mastering" the YouTube platform, and learning how to maximize your potential for success on this very large platform. Additionally, all the topics that will be covered in this section will be incredibly important to consider during all of the later chapters when attempting to gain a complete understanding of the concepts and ideas that will be discussed within these chapters and the rest of this book. As with all sections and individual chapters contained within this book, its sections and chapters will be important steps toward the lofty goal of building your business and becoming successful on YouTube.

Chapter 5: Content Type and Output

The section on "preparation" will be all about all of the various decisions that you will need to make before the actual step of creating each your videos on an individual basis as well as all of the content that you create for your channel on YouTube as a whole. As far as this specific chapter goes, the goal will be to attempt to determine the specific type of content that you will create for your YouTube channel, as well as the duration of each of your videos and the specific amount of content you will create and upload to your channel.

These will all be very important details to consider, as keeping a consistent schedule can make your content more easily accessible. Consistency is important to maintain, both in frequency and the duration of your videos, in order to keep viewers as well.

Once you have developed a clear picture of the type of content that you would like to create and the audience that you will be catering this content to, you will then need to determine the more specific details about your product. Are you aiming for daily vlog updates, or more specifically, targeted content? You will need to find a specific style that fits in well with your established brand. Do you want to create videos on a monthly or weekly basis? You might even choose to post multiple videos per day if you have longer video series projects to produce in multiple parts. In addition to this, you will also need to determine the type of content you would like to create. In order to do this, you will need to use the knowledge of the topics from this book's first section—about gaining a complete understanding of conceptual topics, such as your brand, audience, and niche to further develop your "product." You will need to consider the attitudes, mannerisms, and general persona that you would like to wield in your videos, based on what your audience best responds to.

Once you have determined that and decided on what kind of videos you would like to create, you will need to decide on how long these videos should be. Obviously, you can make exceptions and alter this for certain occasions, or even vary your video lengths regularly, depending on the type of videos you make and how often you will upload these videos. If you only produce occasional update videos, you might want to make them a little bit longer. If you produce weekly or daily videos, then you might decide that 10 or 30 minutes is a good time. It is all about what the best duration is for your viewers to consume easily. You might not think video length would be an important factor. Over the years, however, YouTube has changed its algorithm and the ways it functions and sorts the large amounts of content held within the platform. YouTube no longer likes shorter videos, and allows you to insert another ad break at the 10-minute mark. As such, most content creators usually choose to aim for a duration of 10 minutes or so. This is especially true for those individuals who release daily content. The highest performing YouTube users typically upload multiple videos per day, each slightly longer than 10 minutes each, as videos of this duration are easy to film or record, and allow the highest number of ad breaks as compared to the amount of content, in minutes, that they upload. This allows them to maximize the income that they receive from the monetized content that they upload. It also improves their chances of appearing in search engine results. The average YouTube user spends about 40 minutes per viewing session on YouTube watching videos. If one content creator, for example, uploads three 12-minute videos per day, and a viewer of theirs has an hour for their lunch break, they can watch all three videos. This will increase their page visits from one, if they had uploaded all three videos for the day as one 40-minutes long video, to three separate visits. This will make YouTube, as well as Google, more likely to notice the channel that these videos come from. Optimizing search engine results will be an important part of finding success on YouTube, as being more accessible and easy to find can be an incredibly significant advantage on the internet.

Once you have accomplished these goals and made decisions about the topics that we covered in this chapter, you will be able to move on to the next one. The next chapter in this book's section on preparation will cover whether you should script your videos or choose to improvise the content that you produce.

Chapter 6: Preparing Scripts

Most channels on YouTube that upload on a daily basis, especially ones that put out multiple videos per day, choose to improvise their content. Many of these channels are either daily vlog channels, wherein the host of the channel will simply talk about the day's topic, or "let's play" channels, which focus more on gameplay and commentary provided by the host(s) of the channel. Usually, they will tell stories or talk about the game being played. One example would be in the channel PewDiePie, which currently holds the highest number of subscribers on the platform. The owner and host of the channel, Felix Kjellberg, became popular for playing video games on camera while filming his reactions and commentary to the game he would be playing. This was especially effective and entertaining in the case of horror games. Felix did not enjoy horror, and had wildly expressive reactions to the genre. As such, it became very common for him to upload content involving horror games, as this was the most entertaining to his viewers. He even hosted a TV-style series on YouTube Red, called *Scare PewDiePie*, wherein he would live out the sorts of situations that occur in these video games in real life. Another great example, on the opposite end of the spectrum, is a channel that scripts all of the videos that are created. The host of the most popular YouTube live show on the platform for a time, Matthew Patrick, chooses to go without a script for his live show *Game Theory Live*, but spends days researching topics and carefully scripting each episode of both of his shows, which focus on theories related to popular recreational media, and has even evaluated the algorithms of YouTube itself on his second show, *Film Theory*. Matthew Patrick was involved with theater before creating his show *Game Theory*, and covers topics that are heavily researched before filming. As such, he has decided that the most effective way to run his channel is by writing out scripts for each actual episode whilst improvising on his live show, as it is less specific in its topics and has a lot of surprising or unexpected moments which make that show more entertaining unscripted. This can be an important decision to make, and it really just comes down to what works best for you and the type of content that you wish to create.

Chapter 7: Incorporating Engaging Topics

Once you have developed a clear picture of the specific type of content that you would like to create, the length and frequency of your videos, and whether you should write scripts or not, you should then attempt to find the sorts of topics that you will be covering in your videos. These should be topics that the viewer will find interesting and engaging. This is the reason for "clickbait" videos, as well. While it is not recommended that you create videos that are obviously fake or designed to be "clickbait," you should be attempting to attract viewers with interesting titles and video topics. This can easily be done by finding ways to make the subject matter of your videos fit your audience. You can take the topics that you already have and mold them to your viewers in a way that they will find it enjoyable and feel compelled to watch a video about it. Another good way to accomplish this goal would be to find interesting or engaging topics to cover or discuss about, and then form your videos around those topics. Not everything you create will be of interest to all of your viewers, of course. For instance, topics that may be relevant to you might not be so for those who consume your content. This is why it is important to cater to your audience as much as possible by finding topics that will interest them. If your channel focuses mainly on ads, it is important to consider the people who will be viewing those advertisements. There are also a large number of channels on YouTube that function as "news" outlets and cover drama and other events in various communities, much like the tabloid news website TMZ. These channels are successful, however, because of the more specific and targeted nature of their topics. They typically cover smaller, more closely knit communities or even events surrounding the hosts or owners of other YouTube channels. This works well because most YouTube channel hosts maintain slightly more intimate or personal relationships with their fanbases than those of other media, like the actors on TV shows or radio shows. This helps to get their fans invested in the lives and well-being of the hosts of their favorite channels and allows the people who talk about these topics on their own channels to capitalize on these stories and "news" easily. Many other people choose to tell stories about events that happen in their lives, and some will exaggerate the premise of these stories in the thumbnails or titles for their videos. This can be dangerous, and convince people not to watch your videos if they are repeatedly disappointed by the actual subject matter of the videos when compared to the thumbnail and title. These sorts of "clickbait" videos can dissuade viewers from visiting your channel, so it can be important to watch out and avoid these types of videos. As always, it is up to you to decide how you want to handle this aspect of your content.

Once you have accomplished these goals and made decisions about the topics that were covered in this chapter, you will be able to move on to the next one. The next chapters will be in a separate section of this book, describing the steps to take during the creation process and how to produce interesting and high-quality videos.

Section 3: Creation

Once you have finished the second section of this book, you should have a much clearer understanding of the concepts and ideas that were discussed in that section. These include topics such as determining the type of content that you will include in your videos, the frequency and duration of those videos, the stylistic differences between scripting or improvising content and when one should be favored over the other, and the importance of incorporating engaging topics into your content while keeping in mind the dangers of using deceptive clickbait titles, thumbnails, and descriptions. With this, you should have all of the tools necessary for you to move forward in understanding the concepts that will be covered in the remaining chapters of this book and are well on your way to finding success on YouTube and finding a fulfilling career in content creation.

Rising Stars

This next section is called "creation," and will finally be focusing on how to actually make the videos that you want to create. This section will be about the actual steps you will need to take while producing your content, such as the various parts of the video, which are: The introduction, main section, and end. A majority of this section of the book will focus on these topics and discuss the importance of them, as well as how to go about forming them. The section on creation will also discuss the importance of editing, especially the quality of the editing in both the tools used to do so and the quality of the work. These are very different, and one does not determine the other, after all. The last chapter of this section will be about the importance of a video's thumbnail and how to create good quality thumbnails, regardless of the tools you have available.

These can be important steps on the road to "mastering" YouTube and learning how to maximize your potential for success on the platform. Additionally, the topics to be covered in this section will be important to consider during the later chapters when understanding the concepts and ideas that will be discussed within them. As with all sections and individual chapters contained within this book, this section and its chapters will be important steps toward the lofty goal of building your business and becoming successful on YouTube.

Chapter 8: Introductions

This section will be about the steps to take during the creation process and how to produce interesting and high-quality videos. The chapters in this section will outline the creation of introductions, the main portion, and finally, the endings of each of your videos. Additionally, it will also advise you on how to edit your videos and create thumbnails for YouTube effectively. With these skills, you will be one step closer to maximizing your potential and learning how to build and maintain a successful YouTube channel.

This chapter is about the first part of your video—the introduction. This is what people will see first, and will help them form their "first impressions." During these first few moments, you will need to convince the viewer to continue watching the video. As such, this is arguably the most crucial and sensitive part of each video. Much like how breakfast is the most important meal of the day, and a good (or bad) breakfast can form the basis for the rest of the day, your video's introduction will play a large part in helping the viewer form their opinion of your video and can be vital in convincing the viewer to continue watching. During the introduction stage, you will need to perform a few tasks; The first, as was stated before, is a "hook." This hook should be designed to affect the viewer's first impression of your video. This can be compared to, obviously, your first impression of another person. In your first meeting with another individual, you often decide whether you like them or not, and will base most future encounters with that person on that first impression. Another good way to view this hook stage is to compare it to a "cold open" from your favorite tv show. Usually, these have something to do with the particular episode that they'll be in. Many times, they involve the main characters getting involved in a ridiculous situation that will be interesting to watch, or sometimes this can even show the viewer a glimpse of the episode's climax. Usually, this "cold open" is the execution of an "elevator pitch" for the episode. Sometimes, with "two-part" episodes or the first in a new season, there will be a recap of whatever happened, leading up to the current situation. Really, it's simply a short clip that will explain the events that follow in an interesting way or convince new viewers to continue watching. The best way to come up with a hook for your videos is usually to think of the actual "elevator pitch" that you might make to someone to convince them to watch the video. It works better if you frame it from the perspective of someone who is not involved in the video's creation, as well. Think of things that your target audience, or even people you know, might find interesting and will convince them to want to know more.

The next part of your introduction is going to be referred to here as the "exposition." Once you have gotten past the hook of your video, you need to explain it a little bit more. You should go into a little bit more detail about the topic or topics of your videos. In an instructional video, you should explain what you will help the viewer accomplish, what steps they will be taking, and what tools they might need in order to do so. In an informational video, the exposition stage of your introduction will provide a little bit of information about the topics you will be covering in the video. You might also provide small updates that are relevant to your viewers about your business, or start a brief discussion about current events. The main goal of this part of your video is to form a positive first impression in your viewers, and as the name suggests, introduce the content that will follow in that video. Once you have accomplished these goals and made decisions about the topics that were covered in this chapter, you will be able to move on to the next one.

Chapter 9: Main Content

The section on "creation" will be all about the different individual part of the creation of your videos on an individual basis as well as all of the content that you create in general. As far as this specific chapter goes, the aim will be to figure out how to go about executing the creation of the main portion of each of your videos. This might seem like common sense, but it can be somewhat difficult to know how to proceed at times. Naturally, this is also a very important area to consider when making your videos, as it will be the primary section of all of your videos, and will make up a majority of the content in all of these videos. These factors will be important details to consider during the later chapters of this book, as it will help you to create your content when actually do that.

Once you have finished the first part of your video—the introduction—you will want to probably move on to the next step, in chronological order, which would be the greater part of the video. This will be where you expand on the topics that you ran through in the exposition part of the introduction. This will be where you implement the content that you will have referred to in an "elevator pitch" for the video, like in the introduction. If you introduce new topics that people might not be aware of, you should try to explain them, as some of your viewers might hear you talk about these words or terms but cannot understand what they mean. If this happens, it can impact the accessibility of your videos to the viewer, and might even turn them off your content in some cases.

Many people will choose to use this part of their videos to extend the video's duration as well. Daily vlog or "news" channels are especially guilty of this. As stated before, YouTube allows content creators to add another advertisement break in their videos at the 10-minute mark. This can increase the profit you receive on monetized videos, as it effectively doubles the amount of ad time in your videos, and all you have to do is extend the length of the video by a few seconds. Many channel hosts will do this by explaining the various concepts that they discuss, or even by taking a second to say that they explained a related event or topic in another video, and link that video while doing so. This can be especially helpful to you, as it will present another video for your viewers to watch, possibly extending your channel's watch time even more. Once you have accomplished these goals and made decisions about the topics that were covered in this chapter, you will be able to move on to the next one. The next chapter in the section of this book about "creation" will be about the final part of your videos—the ending.

Chapter 10: Endings

This will be where you "close" each of your videos, recap the topics you covered, possibly recommend other videos to watch, and encourage viewers to communicate or participate in various events. These can be important things to go over, as it can help you to build a sense of community within your viewership and build your audience or create a more dedicated one by making them feel like active participants.

Many people will choose to use this part of their videos to extend the video's duration as well. Many channel hosts will choose to encourage viewers to like the video, make a comment in the video's comment section, and subscribe to the channel in order to get updates about new content from the channel. This can make viewers feel like active participants and become more dedicated to you and your channel. It can also increase the profit you receive on monetized videos, as it effectively doubles the amount of ad time in your videos, and all you have to do is extend the length of the video by a few seconds. Many channel hosts will do this by explaining the various concepts that they discuss or even by taking a second to say that they explained a related event or topic in another video, and link that video while doing so. This can be especially helpful to you, as it will present another video for your viewers to watch, possibly extending your channel's watch time even more.

You could also recommend other videos from your channel for viewers to watch, usually on related or similar topics that they might enjoy. This can be helpful to you and your viewers, as it will possibly increase your watch time, which, of course, is beneficial to you. It can also provide additional videos for your audience, who will then be provided with more entertainment from a channel that they probably enjoy watching content from. All of these tactics can also increase your channel's activity and make you more visible and accessible to your audience as well as to any potential new viewers.

Rising Stars

Once you have accomplished these goals and made decisions about the topics that were covered in this chapter, you will be able to move on to the next one. The next chapter in this book's section on creation will cover another somewhat-related topic. This chapter will be about the filming or recording of your video, and how to best proceed with that.

Chapter 11: Recording

The first aspect of the creation of your videos that you will want to consider is the equipment you use. Many people think that the most expensive or popular tools are the best, and are exactly what they need, but this is not always the case. You can create quality content with simple tools just as effectively as with complex ones. The efficiency is the only thing that changes. The most important thing to consider is which tools you will be able to maximize your efficiency with. Which cameras or microphones or software will be the most useful for the things that you intend to use them for? Video quality is a no-brainer, but many cameras come with different and sometimes even unique features that others might not possess. A lot of the issue is with cost, though. You will need to weigh the cost of the tools you need with the budget that you are comfortable with spending on those tools, as well as the effectiveness of those tools for you and your needs. Software is even more varied. There are many different programs that you might end up using, and many of them require either one-time or monthly payments. There are usually free versions available, but they are typically very simple tools. You can still create high-quality content with these free programs, but it might take a little bit longer than the paid ones, or you might find that they require more steps. It will not be as simple to produce the same content, but you can usually do it with enough creativity.

Chapter 12: Editing

Once you have finished recording, continue that process and edit the raw video content into the final product, which will be what you upload to YouTube.

The first step in the process of editing your videos will be to find the software to edit the videos that you have created. As stated in the previous chapter, there are many different programs that you might end up using, and many of them require either one-time or monthly payments. There are usually free versions available, but they are typically very simple tools. You can still create high-quality content with these free programs, but it might take a little bit longer than the paid ones, or you might find that they require more steps. It will not be as simple to produce the same content, but you can usually do it with enough creativity. The McElroy brothers, who host a series of podcasts that can only be described as an "empire", hosted their own television show based on their first podcast, and two of whom founded the major games journalism company Polygon, have stated multiple times that when they first began to step out into the spotlight with their first podcast, "My Brother, My Brother, and Me", they used simple, cheap microphones from the video game "Rockband". Most content creators have very similar experiences, actually. Almost any channel on YouTube whose host discusses or looks back on the early days of their channel will usually say something about how poor the quality of their videos was at the beginning. This is fine, as there is a learning curve with any skill that you learn, and, creating any sort of content, especially original content, can be very difficult and instill a strong sense of pressure on the person or persons involved.

The next step will be to consider or determine the goal of the video. The way you will edit each video should have a similar vibe as the way you recorded the initial product. This will help you to avoid any sort of dissonance between the two aspects of the video's creation, which would most likely confuse your viewers, and very possibly turn them off that video, or your channel or brand as a whole. As such, it can be very important to keep in mind how your mannerisms can affect the way you edit your content. Things like transition effects or animations can be especially important to keep in mind.

Of course, the final step in this process will be actually to edit the video. This one is very simple. You use the concepts covered earlier in this chapter, the rest of this book as a whole, to polish the raw video you will have recorded by now into a finished, complete product that you will then upload to your YouTube channel. Depending on the tools you are using, of course, this might take a little bit longer than expected. This is fine. As has been stated before, there will be a learning curve. Creating these videos will become much easier with time as you learn all of the tricks to your software that can help the process go by faster. A big hurdle is rendering. Once you've finished editing your video, you will need to save it as a video file again. This process can take a significant amount of time to complete, and you will have to stand by until it finishes, but the good news is that once you reach this part of the process, your work with the video's creation process is done, and you can move on to the next part, which is to create the thumbnail.

Chapter 13: Thumbnails

This chapter will be about how to create a good, high-quality thumbnail for each of the videos that you post on your YouTube channel. YouTube does select specific frames of each of your videos that you can use as thumbnails, but these are usually not the best image for you to use to attract viewers. Sometimes, the thumbnails that YouTube selects for your videos just aren't good enough. In this case, you will want to make your own thumbnails to attach to your videos to make sure that they will be able to easily attract new viewers by catching their eyes and sparking their interest in your videos. Creating a good, eye-catching thumbnail for your videos can instantly grab people's attention. Our brains respond very strongly to striking and attractive visuals, and this can be very helpful for gaining new viewers and to help you stand out from the crowd. This can also help your click-rate, even if people who click on your videos don't stay to watch the whole video. Even just persuading people to click on your videos can help with search engine optimization (SEO) as well, which will be discussed in the chapters on that topic. A boring or uninteresting thumbnail, on the other hand, can even convince people not to click on your videos. This can be detrimental to your channel's growth for similar reasons. Luckily, there are a few tips that you can use to help you to create good thumbnails that will help you to widen your viewership. These methods will be discussed in this chapter and can be found below.

The first thing that you will want to consider about your video's thumbnail is the size of the canvas you have to work with for the thumbnail's image. A 16:9 image aspect ratio is what you will need to use. A 1280 pixels wide and 720 pixels tall canvas works best, and will be the easiest image size for YouTube to use.

It is also important to note that your thumbnail will be used as… Well, a thumbnail. As such, YouTube will shrink the image, so it is important to remember that fact, as you construct the thumbnail. Any text will need to be visible and legible at smaller sizes. This applies to the thumbnail as a whole. You will also want to use bright colors that catch the eye, and simple patterns or textures that can be viewed easily when shrunk down. Most channel hosts choose to use very visible colors for their backgrounds, with a clipping of a relevant image or a frame from the video that fits the theme of the video well, and a short tagline or phrase that will attract attention. There are many websites that will help you construct a good thumbnail for your video, or you can create them manually in a photo-editing program. Both methods work fine, and it depends purely on your preference and the amount of freedom you'd like.

Section 4: Optimization

With this, you should have all of the tools necessary for you to understand the concepts that will be covered in the remaining chapters of this book. You are then well on your way to finding success on YouTube and finding a fulfilling career in content creation.

This next section is called "optimization", and will be focusing on additional skills that will be helpful for you to learn that can be extremely helpful for maximizing (or optimizing) your potential for success in building your channel and brand on YouTube.

Chapter 14: Search Engine Optimization

The section on "optimization" will be all about all of the additional skills that will be helpful for you to learn that can be extremely helpful for maximizing (or optimizing) your potential for success in building your channel and brand on YouTube. This section will be about the steps that you can take in order to maximize your potential on YouTube, such as the basics of search engine optimization and how to effectively manipulate search engines to attract new viewers and build and maintain your audience, and how to build your audience even further by using YouTube as a platform to generate controversy and discourse to encourage interaction within your audience. You can include yourself and use annotations to encourage further interaction within your channel, too. A majority of this section of the book will focus on these topics and discuss the importance of them, as well as how to go about executing them.

As far as this specific chapter goes, the aim will be to go over the basics of search engine optimization. This can be somewhat difficult to understand, and even somewhat daunting at first glance. This chapter will aim to neutralize some of that difficulty by explaining some the ways that you can use your knowledge of search engine optimization to your benefit. Naturally, this will also be a very important area for you to consider when you are making your videos, as it will be the primary section of all of your videos and will make up a majority of the content in all of these videos. These factors will be very important details to consider during the later chapters of this book, as it will help you to actually create your content when doing that.

Search engine optimization, usually referred to as simply "SEO," is very likely a term that you have heard of before. If you have not, then this concept can be described as the process of using the systems of various search engines on the internet to increase the visibility and accessibility of a website or web page. Basically, this is the practice of using search engines to optimize your potential online. This can be a valuable skill in helping you to increase the traffic to your channel and attract new viewers to help build your audience, and in return, your channel on YouTube and your overall brand.

The easiest way for you to go about this process will be first, to consider what your audience may be searching for when they find your channel or your videos if you run a channel based on news or journalism. The most common ways that people find your videos might be to search for videos or other content related to the topics you cover. If you create fictitious content, new viewers might be searching for similar or related content. The most important thing to consider is how people find you on the internet. For a YouTube channel, this is very easy. One way to do this would be to look at your analytics within the platform, and see which of your videos is or are the most popular. These are probably the ones that attract viewers the most. It can also be easy to replicate this as well. In doing so, you will be ensuring the retention of your current viewership too, which will benefit you and your brand in very direct ways. Search engines operate based on keywords. These keywords are what you will need to understand and use to maximize your visibility. These usually include any relevant people, places, objects, or even timeframes. You will want to include these keywords in the tags, titles, and descriptions of your videos in order to benefit from their use.

Once you have accomplished these goals and made decisions about the topics that were covered in this chapter, you will be able to move on to the next one.

Chapter 15: Tags, Titles, and Descriptions

The key to SEO and mastering your proficiency with search engines and the optimization of their systems for your YouTube channel is for you to think in terms of keywords, with regards to the descriptors for your videos. You can do this with any text that is attached to your channel in any way. This can include your channel's various descriptions, as well as the titles, tags, and descriptions of each of the videos on your channel. You will want to use each of these sections to insert these keywords with more detail, and with varying levels of detail as well. The video's tags will each be the actual keywords that you will be using for the video in question. The video's title should be a quick statement or question to catch the attention of a person scrolling by it, and the description should add a little bit more detail, and possibly specific notes about various topics within the video. It is also important to consider that the tags are specifically for search engines to pick up. The title and description will also be helpful for the search engines, but it will be more useful for the viewer.

Once you have accomplished these goals and made decisions about the topics that were covered in this chapter, you will be able to move on to the next one. The next chapter in this book's section on optimization will cover another somewhat-related topic: This chapter will be about the concept of audience retention, how to attract and keep viewers, and how to do this with your newly-learned skills related to search engine optimization. As with all chapters in this book, this chapter will be representative of a very important step toward the lofty goal of building your business and becoming successful on YouTube.

Chapter 16: Audience Retention

The first part of this chapter will be attracting viewers. Of course, this can be very important for you to learn how to do effectively. The topics from the last two chapters, which were SEO and the importance of tags, titles, and descriptions of the videos you post on your channel, will be incredibly helpful for this goal. Accessibility will be a very large portion of this goal, that you will want to pay a lot of attention to during this chapter as well as the previous. Another is to encourage word-of-mouth advertising by encouraging your viewers to participate in events related to the channel or encouraging viewers to share the video with a friend, even. This can be very direct, so it is usually best to do so in more subtle ways. Another good method of attracting viewers and building your audience is to create interesting videos. This seems like a no brainer, but what this really means is to create some sort of controversy or discourse, or create videos that people will actually want to share with others. These sorts of interesting and engaging videos can help to create conversation among your viewers and encourage them to interact with your channel.

The next part of this chapter is audience retention. Audience retention can be described as the act or practice of, of course, retaining or keeping your audience. This is a somewhat-separate topic from attracting viewers in action, but very closely related as the next logical step to take after you have gained the hypothetical follower. In reality, the two will need to be executed at the same time and within each of the videos that you create. Just as with the last part of this chapter, you can encourage interaction from viewers with your channel and videos, and create any sort of controversy or discourse within your content that will wordlessly encourage your viewers to share the video with their friends who might be interested. This will help you build a sense of community for your viewers and to create much more dedicated fans. These are the ones that will eventually help you to build your viewership by word-of-mouth, or by sharing your videos with other people, and who will end up participating in events and discussions related to or about your videos and your channel.

Once you have accomplished these goals and made decisions about the topics that were covered in this chapter, you will be able to move on to the next one.

Chapter 17: Controversy and Discourse

As was mentioned in the last chapter on "audience retention", you will be able to encourage interaction from viewers with your channel and videos. Additionally, creating any sort of controversy or discourse within your content will wordlessly encourage your viewers to share the video with their friends who might be interested in the topic. This will help you to build a sense of community for your viewers and create more dedicated fans. These are the ones that will help you to build your viewership by word-of-mouth or by sharing your videos with other people, and who will participate in events and discussions related to or about your videos and channel. Of course, this can mean many different kinds of things. Controversy, for example, might happen to take the form of an argument or hostility. This can be very easy to accomplish as the result of an accident, and this type of debate is usually better to avoid. This can tend to create a very hostile environment for and within your audience, and can even make the community you create very exhausting or draining to participate in.

Rising Stars

There are a lot of very good examples of individuals and businesses who build communities effectively by sparking debate or discussion among their fanbase. The McElroy brothers, who were mentioned in an earlier chapter of this book, have founded their own company, starred in a television show, and seen success as voice actors in various cartoon network shows. They have built a "podcasting empire" in recent years on the wave of momentum they created out of nowhere—all from a podcast that was initially a simple comedy advice podcast wherein the brothers answered Yahoo! Answers questions on rockband microphones for free. All of their podcasts are actually free, and they receive enough support from their viewership to quit their respective jobs at the company they founded to produce these free podcasts full-time, and even pursue new creative endeavors as they wish, like *The Adventure Zone*, a real-play *Dungeons and Dragons* podcast. This is a show wherein the brothers and their father simply record themselves playing a *Dungeons and Dragons* campaign that Griffin created based on an existing campaign that they played as a placeholder episode for another show, and turned into its own show. Griffin McElroy, the youngest brother, had even been featured on the Forbes 30 Under

Rising Stars

30 list from the year 2017. The McElroys have made many impressive achievements in recent years, and this is largely due to their impressive and astonishingly effective use of word-of-mouth advertisement and their "no bummers" mentality. The McElroys try at all times to keep their "no bummers" rule, which, in basic terms, means that they usually try to remain as positive as they can on their shows, so as to avoid any possible negativity that might come as a result of any "bummer" topics. They also happen to have a very diverse audience, and try very hard to be as accepting as they can be, and to portray that acceptance to their listeners.

On the other end of the spectrum is a popular performance artist named Sam Hyde. Sam actively seeks to discuss controversial topics as often as possible, and takes very obviously offensive and hostile stances in all of the content that he produces. These opinions are typically meant as a sort of social commentary, however, and are not normally his honest opinions on the topics. He even sometimes goes as far as to take very wildly absurd stances and state opinions that would seem as if no real or practical person would have. This is in an effort to compare them to similar stances that some individuals take, and try to expose them as absurd or ridiculous. Sam Hyde, despite his public appearance, possesses a Bachelor of the Arts degree in film, animation, and video, and uses it to great effect to create very weird and disturbing content that aims to create active discourse. Hyde has been almost hyper-public in these sort of endeavors, and has accomplished many wild and surprising feats such as publishing an actual book entitled "*How to Bomb the US Gov't*". He has even started a Kickstarter campaign for a fake video game that was to take the form of a dating simulation game about the children's TV show *My Little Pony: Friendship is Magic*. This fictitious video game concept was intended by Sam to act as a kind of commentary on the unusual and strongly dedicated following that the *My Little Pony* franchise has gained in adult men, which is obviously very far outside of the show's original target demographic of young children. It also serves as an attempt to criticize the extremely inappropriate sexualization that occurs of characters from various entertainment franchises that are intended to be for audiences of underage children, which can very seriously harm the integrity of these franchises and their original audiences' perceptions of them. Sam Hyde even hosted a

Rising Stars

fake TEDx Talk called "2070 Paradigm Shift" that can be viewed on YouTube, wherein he pulled a kind of "prank" on college students, tricking them into attending a performance at Drexel University, wherein he discussed wildly ridiculous predictions of events that will occur in the future, even citing fake statistics and infographics. This fake Ted Talk was described by Forbes as a satiric impersonation of a "Brooklyn tech hipster". It even received a significant amount of coverage from various media outlets. When Sam was asked about the talk and its purpose, he stated that he did not like Ted Talks, and that he viewed them as "really self-congratulatory."

With all of this in mind, you should be considering the aims and goals of your channel, and use that information to spark any sort of engagement or interaction from your audience that may be relevant to those goals. Once you have accomplished these goals and made decisions about the topics that were covered in this chapter, you will be able to move on to the next one. The next chapter in this book's section on optimization will cover another somewhat-related topic. This chapter will be about encouraging interaction from your viewers with other people, as well as with your videos and your channel as a whole, and how that can be helpful to you and to your channel. As with all chapters in this book, this chapter will be representative of a very important step toward the lofty goal of building your business and becoming successful on YouTube.

Chapter 18: Encouraging Interaction

As was mentioned in the last chapter of this book on controversy and discourse, you can use the skills from the chapter on "growing your viewership and audience retention" to encourage your viewers to interact with your videos or participate in channel events or share the video with their friends who might be interested. This will help you to build a sense of community for your viewers and create more dedicated fans. These are the fans that will help you to build your viewership by word-of-mouth or by sharing your videos with other people, and who will participate in events and discussions related to or about your videos and channel.

Using the examples from the last chapter, the McElroy brothers have literally been using these sorts of techniques since they first began to step out onto the stage with their first podcast—all the way back in

2010. The premise for their show was that they would answer ridiculous Yahoo! Answers questions with even more ridiculous answers, and they encouraged their listeners to send in questions that they found interesting. Listeners could even ask their own questions to the McElroys themselves. This turned the format for their show from a simple comedy podcast to a sort of conversation, wherein the brothers would offer comedic advice to actual people who asked for it. They've also been very accepting since the start, as well. They have made a few offensive jokes over the years without realizing it, but every time it happened, the McElroy brothers acknowledged their mistakes, apologized, and made active efforts to avoid those types of comments in the future. Their audience has been very diverse from the start, and the brothers make active choices to try to make their listeners feel comfortable and accepted. This enforces the "no bummers" mentality that the brothers always carry, and keep their shows lighthearted and fun as much as possible.

Rising Stars

Again, on the other end of the spectrum, is Sam Hyde. Sam is a diehard performance artist and actively attempts to anger his audience or make them feel uncomfortable with every action he takes, in an effort to create controversy and discourse for the sake of social commentary. Hyde sports a bowl cut that he claims to be incredibly proud of, and makes jokes dependent on the subversion of common tropes that can be found in everyday life. All his actions are calculated and designed to be controversial, which helps to encourage interaction from both people who do not understand the ironic nature of these actions and become angry, or people who do understand and either become angry or contemplate the meaning behind his videos and actions.

With all of this in mind, you should be considering the goals and aims of your channel and using that information to spark any sort of engagement or interaction from your audience that may be relevant to those goals. Once you have accomplished these goals and made decisions about the topics that we covered in this chapter, you will be able to move on to the next one. The next chapter in this book's section on optimization will cover another somewhat-related topic. The chapter will be about using YouTube's annotations to encourage interaction from your viewers with other people, as well as with your videos and your channel as a whole, and how that can be helpful to you and your channel. As with all chapters in this book, this chapter will be representative of a very important step toward the lofty goal of building your business and becoming successful on YouTube.

Chapter 19: Annotations

Annotations are really interesting, though not something you see a lot lately. The annotations on YouTube are clickable images or text that can be placed in your videos at specific times to encourage viewers to take action—which is usually to click on the annotation. They can appear as text boxes, images, or even video previews, and can contain links to other web pages or simply provide information within text. These are different from the end cards that are used on YouTube in that they can be placed at any time but do not work for mobile users. Annotations can only be viewed on the desktop sites. There are several types of annotations that you can use in your videos:

Speech Bubbles: These speech bubble annotations appear at the top of your videos at the specified times and can be very useful in conveying extra information or the thoughts of the YouTuber.

Notes: Notes are a great way to add extra information as well, but can also be used more freely than speech bubbles and can include links to other web pages or videos. They appear as black or white text on colored backgrounds, and can be set with various text, sizes, colors, placements, timings, and durations within your video.

Title Cards: Title cards do exactly what they say on the box. They are useful for creating title cards in your videos. They are extremely limited, though, and most individuals choose to create their own custom title cards manually.

Spotlights: Spotlight annotations display custom messages when the viewer scrolls their mouse over its area. These can be useful for creating interactive end cards.

Labels: Much like spotlight annotations, labels show custom text when the viewer scrolls over it. They are different, however, as the text appears below the defined area.

Pause: The pause function is less of an annotation and more of a direct playback feature. These will temporarily pause the video for a predetermined amount of time. This allows viewers time to understand a particular frame or read other annotations.

With all of this in mind, you should be considering the goals and aims of your channel, and use that information to spark off any sort of engagement or interaction from your audience that may be relevant to those goals. Once you have accomplished these goals and made decisions about the topics that were covered in this chapter, you will be able to move on to the next one. The next section of this book will be called "capitalization", and will cover another somewhat-related topic. The chapter will be about using YouTube's annotations to encourage interaction from your viewers with other people, as well as with your videos and your channel as a whole, and how that can be helpful to you and to your channel. As with all chapters in this book, this chapter will be representative of a very important step toward the lofty goal of building your business and becoming successful on YouTube.

Section 5: Capitalization

This next section is called "capitalization", and will be focusing on additional skills that will be helpful for you to maximize your potential for success in building your channel and brand on YouTube. This section will be about the process of monetization of your videos, the YouTube streaming service referred to as "YouTube Live" and its various nuances, long-term projects and how they can help you, and useful skills to maintain momentum to keep your channel going. A majority of this section of the book will focus on these topics and discuss the importance of them, as well as how to go about executing them.

 These can be important steps on the road to "mastering" YouTube and learning how to maximize your potential for success on the platform. Additionally, the topics to be covered in this section will be important to consider during the later chapters to understand the concepts and ideas that will be discussed within them.

Chapter 20: Monetization

The section on "capitalization" will be all about all of the skills that will be helpful for you to learn that can be extremely helpful for maximizing (or optimizing) your potential for success in building your channel and brand on YouTube. This section will be about the steps that you can take to maximize your potential on YouTube in this way, such as the the monetization of your videos and how that process works, the YouTube streaming service referred to as "YouTube Live" and its various nuances, long-term projects and how they can help you, and useful skills to maintain momentum to keep your channel going. A majority of this section of the book will focus on these topics and discuss the importance of them as well as how to go about executing them.

Monetization is, to put simply, the act of using various methods in order to gain some profit from your videos. The simplest method of monetization on

YouTube is from advertisement revenue. This will give you a small amount of profit from various advertisements embedded in your videos. If a viewer of yours is a YouTube Premium subscriber, they will not see the ads on your videos. A portion of their monthly YouTube Premium payment, however, will go to your channel in place of the advertisement revenue. There are also channel memberships, which allow your viewers to make recurring monthly payments or donations to you in exchange for exclusive services. You can use shops to sell branded merchandise from your channel as well. Each of these features has a different set of requirements, however, and you will have to reach those goals before you can enable them.

In order to monetize your content on YouTube, you have to reach a number of goals that YouTube uses as requirements for the monetization features. The YouTube Partner Program, which is how channels are monetized, allows YouTubers to "partner" with a company of choice, and thus become associated with it. As such, these channels that become a part of the program need to be held to a higher standard. The first thing that you should note regarding monetization is that all forms of monetization on YouTube require the channel's owner to be at least 18 years of age before they can enable these features, or at least have a parent or guardian over 18 years of age who can handle the payments for you. You must also create appropriate content that meets the standards for YouTube's advertiser-friendly content guidelines. These guidelines are for the content that can be monetized, and advertisers can place ads on them. The FAQ can be found in the Google support site, at https://support.google.com/youtube/answer/91944 76, which outlines all of the content that they will not allow to be monetized on the platform. For the other features, such as the "Merchandise Shelf" and "Channel Memberships", you also need to have a certain number of subscribers to ensure that your channel is active enough for these features to become necessary, and you also need to maintain a clean channel that does not have any YouTube community guideline strikes. To enable the "Merchandise Shelf" on your channel, you need to have at least 10,000 subscribers, and to enable "Channel Memberships", that number jumps to 30,000 subscribers.

Of course, anyone who has a channel on YouTube can easily apply to become a part of the YouTube Partner Program, but there are specific guidelined that YouTube uses to judge whether a channel is fit for their partner program and for monetization. The first thing you will need to do when you apply for the YouTube Partner Program will be to verify whether or not your channel actually meets all of the policies and guidelines that a partnered channel has to abide by in order to be eligible. When you apply, your channel will be submitted and reviewed based on standard procedures that match the ones that were discussed in this chapter. Only a channel that meets these guidelines can be accepted into the YouTube Partner Program. They also check up on various channels that have been accepted into the partner program to make sure that they still meet all of the guidelines and policies that are required for the program.

You will want to make sure that you have an AdSense account to connect to your YouTube account. If you already have one that you can use, you can easily connect it to your channel on YouTube, as long as it has been approved. You are allowed to link multiple channels to a single AdSense account as well. If you have multiple channels, you do not need another AdSense account. You should try to make sure that you only have one account with Adsense. If you do not already have an account with Adsense, you will be able to create one at the time of your application for the YouTube Partner Program. This will not affect the eligibility of your account for the YouTube Partner Program at all.

Additionally, you will need to make sure that your channel has a collective amount of watch-hours equal to or greater than 4,000. If your videos' watch time does not meet this minimum of 4,000 hours, you will not be approved for the YouTube Partner Program. The minimum subscriber count for your channel to be approved for the partner program is 1000, as well. You will need to meet both of these criteria. Otherwise, your channel will be declined. The reasons for these requirements are that if you do not have a consistent viewership, then monetization will not be cost effective on YouTube's side, and they will not be inclined to allow that channel to join their partner program. Additionally, they will need to have a good idea of the (different) kinds of content that your channel produces. If your channel has already reached these requirements, it will normally mean that your channel has a sufficient amount of content for YouTube to judge as accurately as possible for the purpose of determining the channel's eligibility. This will help YouTube to make a much more informed decision regarding its partner program's guidelines.

Additionally, you are allowed to apply for the YouTube Partner Program even if you do not meet these guidelines on your channel's follower and subscriber counts, but your channel will not be reviewed for eligibility until you do meet the minimum threshold for these criteria, at which point YouTube will be evaluated and taken into consideration for the program. In order to actually apply for the YouTube Partner Program, you simply need to sign in to your channel's account on YouTube. Once you have done this, you can select your account's icon in the top right hand portion of the screen within the YouTube website and click on the section called "Creator Studio" within the menu that appears. Once you have completed this step and the webpage loads, you will be able to see another menu on the left side of the screen. Within that menu, you can find and click on the "Channel" option. This will lead to a sort of drop-down menu with another option called "Status and Features," which you will also want to click on. The Status and Features section will lead you to a menu with an option for "Monetization." If you find this option, you can then click on a switch that says "Enable," which will then cause a prompt to appear on your screen. At that point, you simply need to follow the steps that appear and wait for your account to be reviewed and considered for eligibility.

If your account already meets all of the eligibility requirements for the YouTube Partner Program, It will be placed in a queue for reviewing. If it does not, it will be placed in the queue once it does meet these requirements. Once the queue reaches your channel's spot, your channel will be evaluated by a combination of YouTube's automated systems and human evaluators in order to determine whether the content on your channel meets YouTube's requirements and guidelines. YouTube will respond to your application for its partner program once your account has been evaluated to determine its eligibility, which usually takes about one month. Of course, there are certain exceptions and various situations that can cause extended wait times, such as an unusually high number of applications for YouTube to review issues that can occur within their systems, or even a shift in systems or the resources used for these purposes. You will be able to check on your application's status at any time, however. And if your account is determined to be ineligible, it isn't the end of that matter. You will be able to apply again in another 30 days after your account is declined for the partner program, and there are even resources that can help you to strengthen your eligibility and boost your likelihood of being approved.

With all of this in mind, you should be considering the goals and aims of your channel and use that information to spark any sort of engagement or interaction from your audience that may be relevant to those goals. Once you have accomplished these goals and made decisions about the topics that we covered in this chapter, you will be able to move on to the next one. The next chapter of this book will cover another somewhat-related topic. This chapter will be about using YouTube's "Live" service to host live shows and allow viewers to stream live content from your channel, as well as how that can be helpful to you and to your channel. As with all chapters in this book, this chapter will be representative of a very important step toward the lofty goal of building your business and becoming successful on YouTube.

Chapter 21: YouTube Live

With the recent surge in the popularity of streaming services like Twitch and Rabbit, YouTube has also created its own service to allow its users to stream live content to their viewers. With YouTube Live, you can stream content with to your viewers as it's filmed. This feature allows for a more personal conversation with your viewers, and gives you another way to produce high-quality and entertaining content for viewers to enjoy. Just as with your monetized content, however, there are a few things that you need to do before you can set up this service for your channel. The first prerequisite for using the YouTube Live service is to verify your YouTube channel. After that, you will need to make sure that you do not have any channel live stream restrictions from the past 90 days. Once you have met these criteria, you simply need to enable the YouTube Live streaming service. This can be done very easily by going to the "Creator Studio

Tools" menu in your channel settings and selecting the "Live Streaming" option.

Once you have enabled this feature as described above, you can create a new stream. This can be done in one of three ways:

Stream Now: You can select this option to begin streaming in a very quick and easy way. Begin the stream to start broadcasting your content, and YouTube will automatically start and stop the stream for you at the correct time.

Events: This function gives you more tools to allow you to have more control over your live streams. You will be able to stop and start your streams as you wish.

Mobile: This will allow you to stream from the mobile application.

These different types of streams will provide slightly different services, and you can play with them to decide which will be best for your current purpose.

You will even be able to implant your YouTube Live stream on another web page. In order to do this, you will need to have an endorsed AdSense account connected to your YouTube channel. The process of beginning and hosting YouTube Live streams is quite easy, and with the booming prevalence YouTube Live TV, it's only going to be more popular as well.

With all of this in mind, you should be considering the goals and aims of your channel and using that information to spark any sort of engagement or interaction from your audience that may be relevant to those goals. Once you have accomplished these goals and made decisions about the topics that were covered in this chapter, you will be able to move on to the next one. The next chapter of this book will cover another somewhat-related topic. This chapter will be about using YouTube's various features as well as taking your own initiative in order to maintain momentum. This can also take the form of another good skill to learn and manage, which is to create long-term projects and video series, as well as how that can be helpful to you and to your channel. As with all chapters in this book, this chapter will be representative of a very important step toward the lofty goal of building your business and becoming successful on YouTube.

Chapter 22: Maintaining Momentum

The concept of "maintaining momentum" can sometimes be difficult, as there aren't actually any concrete methods that you can employ in order to do it. The issue with this topic is that it is largely reliant on you and your ability to keep yourself motivated. Of course, there are many different ways that you can keep yourself motivated, but on YouTube, specifically, there are a number of ways that you can do this. One way, as with most endeavors, is that you can create a schedule for yourself if you make sure to upload a video at a set pace. Of course, there can be exceptions, but they should be kept at a minimum, if at all possible. Many YouTube channel hosts choose to adopt the pattern used by television shows, and will typically upload one video every week, on a set day of the week. This can not only allow you to maintain your own schedule and keep a steady pace, which will make it easier for you to consistently create content and form a habit out of this new schedule, but it will also make your videos more accessible for your viewers. "Maintaining momentum" does not just mean keeping yourself motivated, however. Another large part of this is keeping your channel alive and active. If you make sure to keep a consistent schedule for your channel, your subscribers will be able to predict a new video releasing and will know to check your channel at the prescribed time, which will increase the number of views on that video. This will, in turn, show up in your analytics, and YouTube will automatically see that your channel is receiving a spike of attention on a certain day at a certain time and will use that information. This tells YouTube's system that people are interested in your channel at a specific day and time, and YouTube will then use that information to recommend your videos to individuals who might be interested in your video or videos at that time. This will allow your channel to maintain relevance and keep views before your scheduled video is even uploaded. There are a few ways that you can help yourself to stay motivated, even on rough days or during times that you might not feel particularly inclined to move forward with the goals that you have set for yourself. These methods can help you to avoid experiencing a sort of "burn out," and are listed below:

- Set specific goals that are very easy for you to visualize in detail. If you set concrete and attainable goals for yourself, this can help you feel motivated to achieve these goals. You should be able to visualize your goals in detail. If you can visualize your goals and the results of accomplishing those goals, it will become much easier to reach. A simple goal point that you feel like you can easily accomplish will be much easier than one that is far off, or one that might seem intimidating or impossible to you. It can also be very helpful to understand this concept with the context of athletes and their performance. If a person is trying to run a specific distance, such as a mile or a 5-kilometer run, they will usually tend to break up the total distance into shorter increments, like a number of laps around a track, or a specific section of the track. This way, you only need to run one lap four times, or one kilometer five times. This can make the overall goal much less intimidating and easier to achieve in the long run.

- Make lists of all of the reasons that you want to accomplish your goals. If you do not know why you are attempting to accomplish a specific goal, it can be very easy for you to lose motivation and to fall off course. For this reason, it can be very important to sort of "ground" yourself and remember why you need to or want to accomplish a specific goal. You can set goals for yourself all you like, but if you do not have a good reason for reaching these goals to help keep you on track, it can be too easy for you to give up and abandon these goals simply. You might even want to make a list of specific points and different reasons that these goals will help you. If you do so, however, you should try to physically write these lists out with a pen and paper, as opposed to typing them on your phone or computer. Since typing is a much more "automatic" process that only goes as deep as selecting specific letters to form words, you aren't as engaged when you write your lists this way. When you use a pen to write the words that you are thinking physically, your brain will be more actively engaged and focused on the words that you are writing.

- Break your goals down into small segments to make accomplishing them seem less intimidating. This can help you to stay more motivated by creating much smaller goals that are easier for you to reach, and various milestones for you to reach along the way as well. As was stated before, if you only have one very large goal to reach, it can become intimidating. It will then become much easier for you to become intimidated and lose focus. If you try to accomplish your overall mission as a whole right away, it will almost certainly become overwhelming. However, if you "chip away" at this overarching goal and break it down into smaller, much more realistic steps, you can then do one at a time and move on to the next section. When you reach each small milestone, your brain will activate its "reward center" and release small amounts of dopamine, which can provide a little reward for reaching these milestones. This can also help to keep you focused and inspired to continue to move forward to the next step as well.

- Learn to be flexible and open to new situations. You should always have a strategy planned out regarding any goals that you have set for yourself, but you should also try to be flexible and open when things don't always work out in the ways that you might expect them to. Thomas Edison once said, "I have not failed. I have just found 10,000 ways that won't work." Failure is, in this way, a fallacy. You can not fail simply by not managing to reach a specific goal. The only possible way that you can fail in any task is to admit defeat and give up. Until you do that, you can still try again and keep going forward until you succeed.

- Don't be afraid to get help if you need it. If you need or want help to accomplish any goals that you set for yourself, you should not be afraid to ask or accept this help. It does not necessarily need to be a very big issue, but even if you might theoretically be able to accomplish your goals on your own, there is a sort of value inherent in accepting outside help. Many people will be too "proud" or stubborn to allow themselves to accept help from other people and to be seen as weak or incapable of accomplishing their goals.

Accepting help and sharing your plans with others can even be helpful. An outside opinion can help you to gain a new perspective on the situation and can make accomplishing your goals that much easier. It might also be the case that you do not have a particular set of skills that are necessary in order for you to accomplish your goals, in which case you might need to seek additional help from someone who is able to help in that way. On the other hand, however, you should avoid being too "picky" about getting help from other people. You should be open to different options, as well, while still making a point to make sure that if you accept help from an outside source, they should be able to assist you in accomplishing the goals that you have set.

- Understand how you should handle burnout. Everyone eventually faces burnout, and when this comes, you should know how to deal with it. It is almost an inevitability that at some point, you will encounter some sort of setback or exhaustion that can cause you to lose motivation for a period of time. When this happens, you might need a little boost to help you overcome it and continue to be motivated and keep moving forward with your goals. You can do this in several ways which work differently for different people. Some might tend to think about other situations that other people have endured in the past in order to accomplish their goals. Others might even return to a list of reasons they want to accomplish their goals or set rewards for themselves once they accomplish these goals in order to continue to stay motivated as much as possible. Any method that works for you in order to help you to push past this kind of burnout will be incredibly helpful to keep you on the right track. Regardless of what methods you use to help you in doing this and accomplishing the goals that you set for yourself, Winston Churchill can serve as an excellent role model. Winston Churchill was once invited to speak to a group of students, to whom he gave an especially inspiring speech. Within that speech, he uttered a very inspirational and useful quote; "Never, ever, ever, ever, ever, ever, ever give up."

- Periodically remind yourself of your motivations. This will also be incredibly helpful in avoiding any sort of burnout. If you revisit a list, you may have made a reminder of the reasons that you actually want or need to accomplish a specific goal. This can help you to stay on track much more reliably and consistently. You might face setbacks or a lack of motivation in trying to accomplish a daunting task, and when this happens, you need to continue to move forward.

With all of this in mind, you should be trying to actively consider all of the goals and aims of your channel, and using that information to spark any sort of engagement or interaction from your audience that may be relevant to those goals. Once you have accomplished these goals and made decisions about the topics that were covered in this chapter, you should have all of the tools necessary to allow you get the most out of YouTube and maximize your potential, as well as the potential of your business and your brand on the platform. As with all chapters in this book, this chapter will be representative of a very important step toward the lofty goal of building your business and becoming successful on YouTube. *How To Grow Your Audience, Your Business, And Your Revenue By Creating Captivating Videos About Your Everyday Life With YouTube Marketing* is designed to guide you on how to understand your brand and target audience and use that knowledge along with the knowledge of your product and the type of content that you are aiming to put out, to help you formulate interesting and engaging videos that will attract and keep consistent, dedicated viewers and follower bases in order to find a foothold in the YouTube market. This will allow you to eventually carve out your own path, and from there, build a legitimate career in content creation.

Conclusion

Congratulations! By this point, you should have finished another last section of *How To Grow Your Audience, Your Business, And Your Revenue By Creating Captivating Videos About Your Everyday Life With YouTube Marketing (With Actionable Tips To Follow From Successful YouTubers)*! You should now have a much clearer idea of the concepts that were covered within that final section, such as the monetization of your videos and how that process works, the YouTube streaming service referred to as "YouTube Live" and its various nuances, long-term projects and how they can help you, maintaining momentum to help you keep your channel going, as well as why these can be such useful and important skills. With this, you will have completed the final chapter of this book, and should have all of the tools necessary to allow you to "master" YouTube and to learn how to maximize your potential for success on the platform and create a fulfilling career in content creation for yourself as well as to build your brand and business.

This can be a very difficult, time-consuming, and mentally exhausting task, but *How To Grow Your Audience, Your Business, And Your Revenue By Creating Captivating Videos About Your Everyday Life With YouTube Marketing* is designed to help you with this goal by acting as a guide on how to understand YouTube's system and its various tools and functions, as well as a number of different, incredibly helpful skills, to help you to attract and keep consistent, dedicated viewers and follower bases in order to find a foothold in the YouTube market and eventually carve out your own path, and from there, build a legitimate career in content creation.

Connect with us on our Facebook page

www.facebook.com/bluesourceandfriends and stay tuned

to our latest book promotions and free giveaways.